This book belongs to:

....

FRIENDLY FARM ANIMALS

HAVING FUN!

· Share-A-Book ·

At daybreak the rooster crows, "cock-a-doodle-doo," signaling the beginning of a day on the farm.

The hen and her chicks scratch and peck
for corn in the barnyard.

"Cluck, cluck," say the chickens.

A turkey struts around the barnyard
showing his colorful feathers.

"Gobble, gobble," says the turkey.

Near the barn, the little donkey stands waiting for hay.

"Hee-haw," says the donkey.

The mother duck takes a bath as she watches her ducklings.

"Quack, quack," say the ducks.

On the farm pond, the ducklings swim
and dive for food.

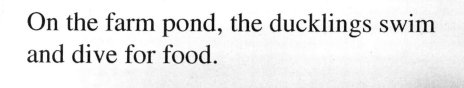

The lamb's mother rests in the sunshine.

"Baa, baa," say the ewe and her lamb.

A young lamb looks over
the green grass in the pasture,
ready to graze.

The mare trots after her colt.

In a nearby pasture, a colt frolics in the sun.

Out in the pasture is a cow and her calf. The calf is exploring the flowers.

"Moo, moo," say the cow and her calf.

The mother pig enjoys rolling in the cool mud in the hog pen while her piglets play nearby.

"Oink, oink," say the pigs.

A goat leaps across the pasture to graze with the other farm animals.

It's always fun on the farm!

**Look for other
titles in this series:**

Beautiful Zoo Animals
Furry Wild Animals
Incredible Dinosaurs

Mount Saint Helens is a kind of volcano
called a composite volcano.
Composite volcanoes are made
of many layers of lava, rock, and ash.
Most volcanoes around the world
are composites.

Mount Fuji in Japan, Mount Vesuvius
in Italy, and Mount Shasta in California
are composite volcanoes.
They all have steep sides.
And they often blow apart
without much warning.

A New Volcano

One February day in 1943,
a farmer was busy working in his field.
He lived in a Mexican village
called Paricutin.
He and his family had been feeling
strong earthquakes for weeks.
On this day,
the farmer heard a loud noise.
The noise sounded like thunder.
He looked up and saw a clear sky.
No storm was in sight.

Thunder rumbled again.

Everything shook.

Then the ground in front of the farmer
swelled and cracked open.

Dust and steam rose from the crack.

A hissing noise grew louder and louder.

The farmer became frightened.

He moved a safe distance away.

After he did,

hot lava shot high into the air.

The lava cooled as it fell to the ground.
It hardened and broke into small pebbles
called cinders.
Trapped inside the cinders
were bubbles of gas.
The bubbles made the cinders
look like glass.
They piled up around the
vent in the ground.

More lava burst from the volcano.

The lava flowed toward two villages.

Soon the villages were buried.

Dust and red-hot ash also burst
from the volcano.

The ash covered forests nearby.

The pile of cinders grew taller and taller.
At the end of one year, the volcano was the
size of a building with one hundred floors.
The volcano erupted for eight more years.
But it did not grow much.
Finally, one day it stopped hissing,
rumbling, and spitting.
The village named the volcano Paricutin.
Paricutin is a kind of volcano
called a cinder cone volcano.
It is the first cinder cone volcano
that anyone had ever seen being formed.

Many other cinder cone volcanoes
are in the western part of North America.
All of them are in the shape of cones
built with layers of cinders and ash.
They are much smaller
than composite volcanoes.
Lassen Peak in California, Craters of the
Moon in Idaho, and Sunset Crater
in Arizona are all cinder cone volcanoes.

Island of Fire

On the night of March 24, 1984,
small earthquakes shook
the Big Island of Hawaii.
Then a large earthquake struck
early the next morning.
People saw in the distance
a bright red glow in the sky.
It looked like the rising sun.

The glow was coming
from a wide mountain called Mauna Loa.
The largest volcano on Earth
had begun to erupt.

Lava spilled out of the top of Mauna Loa.

The hot liquid slowly flowed

down the volcano's sides.

It covered them

with layer upon layer of lava.

Fountains of lava also burst up from other

openings around the mountain.

The hot liquid set plants blazing nearby.
The burning plants filled the air
with sparks and smoke.
The lava moved over highways
and toward the city of Hilo.
Everyone waited and wondered.
Would the city be buried
under the liquid fire?

The lava flow slowed down
before it reached Hilo.
By April 14, the lava had stopped
flowing out of some parts of the volcano.
Mauna Loa's eruption ended
the next day.
Since then, the volcano has been quiet.

Mauna Loa is a kind of volcano
called a shield volcano.
Shield volcanoes have wide sides.
The sides are shaped like the rounded
shields of warriors.
All of the Hawaiian Islands
formed from shield volcanoes.
These volcanoes begin thousands of feet
under the sea.
They are the largest mountains on Earth.
Iceland has other shield volcanoes
that formed in the same way.

Volcanic Activity

About 50 to 70 volcanoes
erupt around the world each year.
Volcanoes that are erupting all the time
are active volcanoes.

Kilauea in Hawaii is an active volcano.

Its last eruption began in 1983.

Lava is still flowing out of it.

No one is sure when it will stop.

Volcanoes that have been sleeping
for many years are dormant volcanoes.
But they could erupt again.
Mount Etna in Italy and Popocatepetl
in Mexico were dormant for many years.
Then they exploded
and became active once more.

A volcano that has not erupted for
thousands of years is an extinct volcano.
Mount Kenya in Africa
is an extinct volcano.
It is not expected to blow its top
any time soon.

Changing the Earth

Volcanoes can be terrifying.
They have destroyed cities
and killed people.
But volcanoes can also be good
for life on Earth.
They have formed many islands,
mountains, and parts of continents.

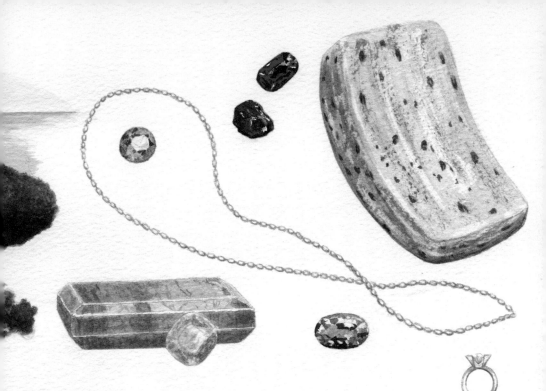

Lava rocks help build roads.

Beautiful stones from volcanoes
are turned into jewelry.

Pumice is a natural glass made from lava.

It can grind and polish stones
and metals.

Pumice is also used in making
hand soaps and household cleaners.

People in some places turn heat
from volcanoes into energy for electricity.
The electricity lights homes and offices.
It runs televisions and other machines.
Rocks and ash from volcanoes.
are good for farming soil.
Vines, vegetables, and flowers planted
in this soil grow better
than they do anywhere else.

That is why people continue to live
and work near dangerous volcanoes.
But someday the volcano
may awake again.
Then everyone must be ready
to run for safety.

Studying Volcanoes

Imagine being on an active volcano. Lava is bubbling out of several small holes. You walk closer to one of the holes. A blast of heat makes you turn away. The smell of rotten eggs fills the air. Suddenly, the ground shakes. You feel as if you are going to fall. This is a dangerous place. But some scientists actually work here.

These men and women are called volcanologists. They study active volcanoes. Some of the volcanologists collect gas, rock, or ash samples from around vents. They wear helmets and masks for protection. Others dress in firefighters' shirts and boots. They walk across lava and measure its temperature. Some scientists even stand near fountains of fire during an eruption. They record what is happening.

Other scientists set up special equipment and cameras. A few fly over volcanoes in helicopters. They take pictures and report where lava is heading.

Volcanologists try to understand everything about volcanoes. They want to make life safer for the people living and working nearby.

Glossary

Cinder cone volcano (SIHN-der COHN vahl-KAY-noh): A volcano built up almost completely by pebble-sized pieces of lava called cinders

Composite volcano (cahm-PAH-ziht vahl-KAY-noh): A steep cone-shaped volcano built up by layers of lava, rocks, and ash

Crater (CRAY-tehr): Bowl-shaped land around a volcano's vent

Dormant volcano (DOHR-mahnt vahl-KAY-noh): A volcano that is sleeping but may soon become active

Erupt: (EE-ruhpt): To flow or burst out the way lava rushes from a volcano

Extinct volcano (ek-STEENCT vahl-KAY-noh): A volcano that has not erupted for thousands of years

Lava (LAH-vah): Melted rock from a volcano

Magma (MAG-mah): Melted rock still inside Earth

Plates (PLAYTS): Layers of rock beneath Earth's land and sea that fit together like pieces of a jigsaw puzzle

Shield volcano (SHEELD vahl-KAY-noh): A gently sloping volcano formed by flowing lava

Vent (VEHNT): an opening in Earth's crust where melted rock escapes

Volcanologists (Vuhl-keh-NAHL-oh-gihsts): scientists who study volcanoes

Bibliography

Colasurdo, Christine. "Nature Erupts in Spirit Lake's Backcountry."
    Pacific Discovery. 48 (1995): 8–16.
Colasurdo, Christine. "Before the Mountain Blows." *Pacific Discovery.*
    49 (1996): 26–29.
Decker, Robert W., and Barbara B. Decker. *Mountains of Fire: The Nature
    of Volcanoes.* New York: Cambridge University Press, 1991.
Fisher, Richard V., Grant Heiken, and Jeffrey B. Hulen. *Volcanoes:
    Crucibles of Change.* Princeton, NJ: Princeton University Press, 1997.
Francis, Peter. *Volcanoes: A Planetary Perspective.* New York: Oxford
    University Press, 1993.
Pendick, Daniel. "What's This Volcano Trying to Tell Us?" *New Scientist.*
    161 (1999): 26–31.
Robinson, Andrew. *Earth Shock: Hurricanes, Volcanoes, Earthquakes,
    Tornadoes and Other Forces of Nature.* New York: Thames and
    Hudson, 1993.
Scarth, Alwyn. *Volcanoes: An Introduction.* College Station, TX: Texas
    A&M University Press, 1994.
Scarth, Alwyn. *Vulcan's Fury: Man against the Volcano.* New Haven, CT:
    Yale University Press, 1999.
Sigurdsson, Haraldur, ed. *Encyclopedia of Volcanoes.* San Diego, CA:
    Academic Press, 2000.
Thompson, Dick. *Volcano Cowboys: The Rocky Evolution of a Dangerous
    Science.* New York: St. Martin's Press, 2000.